# ΣOFIA BEFORE LOVE

A BOOK OF POEMS

Book Cover and illustrations by Zoë Tavares Bennett.

First edition 2026

ISBN-13: 979-8-9943310-0-2

# ΣOFIA BEFORE LOVE

A BOOK OF POEMS

ZOË TAVARES BENNETT

MEDITERRA PRESS

*To Livia, my sister, most fair of Ocean's daughters.*

φιλοσοφία, ἡ, *philosophy* (noun)

a compound of φίλος, 'love of,' and σοφία, 'wisdom'

# CONTENTS

# Preface

In this ancient-meets-modern composition of my collected poems, I have utilized various metrical and rhyming schemes, everything from traditional iambic sonnets, ballads, and quatrains to more formidable sestina, dactylic hexameters, and alliterative Anglo-Saxon verse, to the elegant, pensive haikus and sparse lines reminiscent of Sappho's fragmentary poetry, interspersed with my own humble illustrations. Named after the obscure figure of Sofia—at once the Ancient Greek σοφία, or "wisdom," but also the name of a woman before she encounters love, or φίλος—in relation both to philosophy but also more generally to maidenhood—these poems explore the ancient wisdom passed down from mother to daughter, interpreted through the fresh, knowledgeable and yet unmoored gaze of the modern woman.

Following the death and rebirth of Persephone, *Sofia Before Love* leads the reader through four related stages as told in the *Homeric Hymn to Demeter*: *Korē*, or "Maiden," the name for Persephone before marriage; *Death*, for her descent to the Underworld after she was seized by Hades and wedded to him; *Wisdom*, gained in the act of eating pomegranate seeds, whether tricked or willingly, and often considered her maturation as a woman; and lastly, *Spring*, the joyful return of Persephone to her mother Demeter, who allows the earth to flower once more. As befits our modern world, these poems slip in and out of different mythological, religious, philosophical, and invented landscapes, fusing well-known Classical legends with Egyptian and Near Eastern myths in metrical styles reminiscent of pagan, Germanic epics or cantering Italian sonnets or even simple, anonymous folk songs one might have heard once whistled by a fair maiden picking flowers...

In the footsteps of poets like J.R.R. Tolkien, whose gaze pierced through that veiled age of prehistory and recalled their songs in familiar meters, I have attempted to gather into one cohesive whole the enchanting, perilous world of Homer, the dreamy, Celtic air of the western edges of Europe, Egypt's austere religiosity and late pagan philosophy, mystical Babylonian skies and stars, and the Abrahamic theology of the Near East, all mingled with reimagined stories in familiar places, translated and invented Ancient Greek hymns, and poetical musings of a girl—Sofia—as she embarks on the ancient and yet still mysterious path of becoming a woman, just like Persephone did before her, and still does each year in the dark depths of Winter before the flowering of Spring.

# KORĒ

*Fragmentary Dreams*

I am going to the land of dreams,
the forgetting of Night.

*Ode to Sofia*

I used to sleep under the stars
When gods kept watch at night
And Sun chased Moon across the sky
Like two love birds in flight.

If then my Fate is bound to Earth
And Spring and Winter herald Death,
Why calls Eternity my name
An icy wind Her divine breath?

Please tell me, Mother, who am I
When snow buries me deep
And Time is a forgotten name
I dream of in my sleep?

Then will you hold me in your arms
And whisper in my ear goodnight?
Can then you call me *Daughter* and
Say everything will be alright?

I used to sleep under the stars
Before the taste of Love.
My body knew without Him all
The deathless gods above.

## *The Garden of Eden*

Across the river, yonder woods and dells
there grows a garden by the endless seas,
where midst the roses, lilies, and bluebells
meander butterflies and buzzing bees.
Amid the garden grows a tree of elm
whose ancient roots delve deep as branches high,
the orchid, tulip, narcissus her realm
as birds above their treetop kingdom fly.
No evil plagues the garden, nor does Death,
for Time itself cannot her grasses tread
nor mortal men shall taste her fragrant breath,
lest trespassing her gates they wind up dead.
Behold! among the flowers running wild—
a fair-faced maiden singing—Nature's child.

*Ode to Jupiter, Deus Pater*

As Night unfurls above the Earth
I lift my eyes on high,
Where shining brightly white I see
A star amid the sky.

At first my gaze does not perceive
Beyond a starlit sea,
But slowly ebb away the clouds
From immortality.

On lofty heights a twinkling eye
Of father sky divine,
Its cold blue light upon my face
Reveals an ancient sign.

Before the cosmic pantheon
*Deus Pater* his name,
A king of kingdoms heavenly
He reigns by wrathful flame.

Yet fatherly his tender brow
Beholding mortal kind,
A race he made with Mother Earth
Imagined like his mind.

Forever shall his will be done
Long after you or me,
For Love betwixt the universe
Will never cease to be.

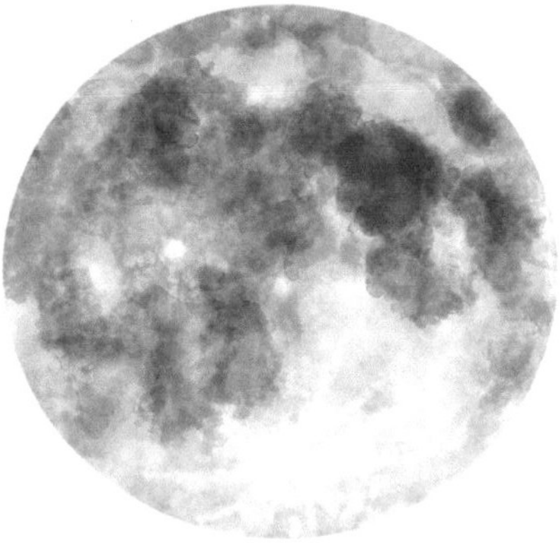

*Moonrise (in Sapphic Stanza)*

Full in the heavens rose the moon with fair tress,
Blushing behind the clouds, she stood unabashed.
Goddess, gray-eyed Selene, of pearls her white dress,
Glancing down, she asked:

“Why do you fret, my child, so young and lithe-limbed?
Soon you will age and death shall snuff you out cold,
Like some flame-burning candle caught in rough wind,
Fate for men age-old!”

“Deathless may gods be, O Selene Menē, please,
Pity me nonetheless!” I begged the night sky.
“Why must men suffer grief and toil and disease?
Moon, be my ally!”

Hearing my plea, the goddess laughed at my plight:
“Fight not against your Fate, for blind is man’s gaze,
Who cannot see beyond his eyes without light!
Trust in that always!”

Doom in my heart befell as shadows veiled Moon,
Mingled with light like silver under Sun’s glare,
Hearing fair voices sing a hymn to some tune
Old as the hills bare.

Long did I look upon the Moon with held breath,
Searching for immortality in cruel Time:
Can my words live forever long after death
Buried in versed rhyme?

*An Ode to Odysseus*

A man of twists and turns, I sing of you,
the wanderer, O Muse tell us
in words too few
of Argive lord, Odysseus,
whose love for her was always true,
though years he sailed across the wine-dark sea,
a love withstanding Time
or any rhyme,
for she who wove and waited, wise Penelope.

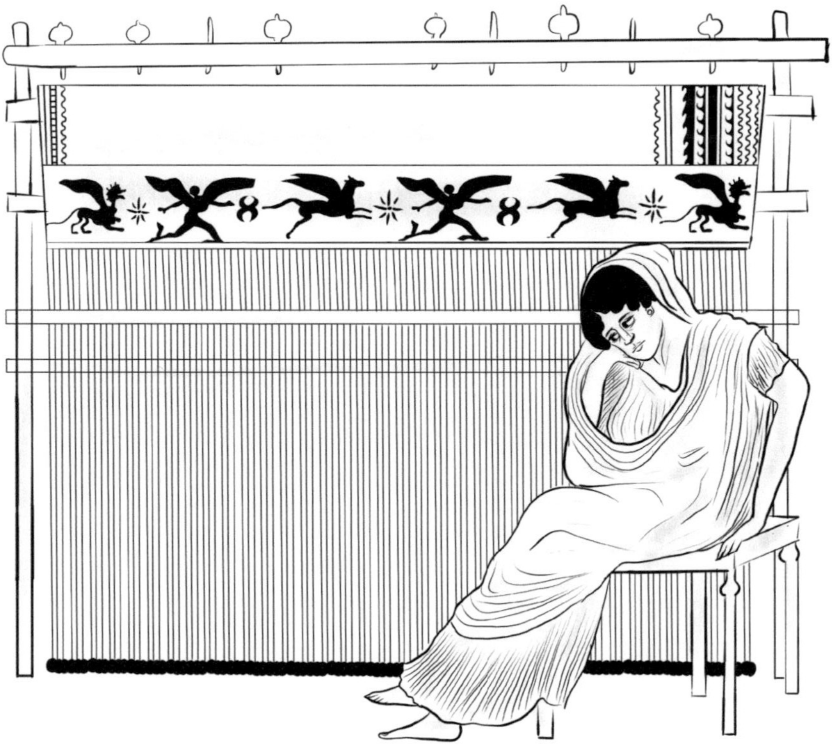

## *A Oliveira*

Leaves of silver trumpet
Branches of satin gray
Fruits be sharp and bitter
Till brine soaks it away.

Pressed for her rich oil
Bygone burnt for her light
Now nary a kitchen
Without it be aright.

But far more beautiful
Than any fruit may be
To see below the moon
A swaying olive tree.

*Terra Romana nella Terza Rima*

An ancient oak sits on the brow of hills,
a sentinel of towns whose roots run deep
like Roman wells and water-wheeling mills.

For ages man did earth's soft soil reap
in Italy where Trojan race fulfills
the will of Juno, settling wrath to sleep,

a land where mingled gods and mortal men,
whose very air can draw the veil of Time
from misty Myth where heroes live again.

Afar afield I hear some church bells chime
as once did ward off ill from Roman doors
a custom old as sunny Latin clime.

In dreams I wash upon your fateful shores,
where long have men for glory fought their wars.

*Verse Translation of the Homeric Hymn to Artemis*

I sing of Artemis with golden shaft,
the loudly sounding august virgin maid,
for deer she shoots and arrow-darts her craft,
the sister to Apollo Golden-blade,
who over shadowed hills and windy peaks,
delights in chase, her golden bow pulled taut,
and sending darts she causes fearful shrieks,
then tremble tops of mountains held aloft,
grim cries of beasts in tangled woodland knoll,
then quakes the earth and sea where fishes shoal.

She bold of heart did wander every way
destroying breeds of beasts to heart's content,
the arrow-pourer spying beasts of prey,
then cheered of mind and slacking bow well-bent,
she goes to lofty home of brother dear,
Apollo Phoebus, in Delphí's rich land,
put Charites and Graces dancing fair.
There unstrung bow and arrows she then hanged,
and leading first with graceful adorned frame,
began the dance, their godly strains exclaim.

They sang of Leto, fair-ankled, who bore
the children best among the gods prevail,
in both their schemes and any endeavor.
O Zeus and fair-haired Leto's children, hail!
I'll keep in mind both you and one song more!

*A Weaving Song*

Take the sheep then grab the shear,
shaving their soft coat,
then wash the wool until it's clear,
making the hairs bloat.

Take the hair then mix the dyes,
stain them red and blue,
then purple, yellow, green likewise,
and even gold flecks too.

Take the wool then fit the spindle,
round the whorl it goes,
then watch your wool slowly dwindle,
making thread for throws.

Take the yarn then warp the beam,
the hanged threads to lock,
then the heddle bar weaves the scheme,
each end weighed by rock.

Take the shuttle then pull the weft,
weave it through the shed,
then beat the sword till no gap's left,
repeat to fill the spread.

Take the ends and tie 'em in knots,
sealing woven thread,
as the Fates seal man's doom in lots,
finished when we're dead!

## Ἀοίδη, *An Original Lyric Poem in Sapphic Greek*

νῦν ἄκουσον, εἶπε, βίω ἀοίδην ·
ὠράνῳ δε ἄστερες αἶψα εὗρει
ἀγλάοι κύκλοισι λέγων τελεύτων
τὸν λόγον ἄρχαν.

γῆ μέλαιν' ἔτος κὰτ ἔκαστον ὔμνει
νόστον ὤρᾳ Περσέφονας σὺν ἄλλοις
χρώμασιν καὶ τῶ θανάτω τὸ ψῦχος
ὠς πάλιν ἔλθοι.

αἰ βρότων φώναι ἐφέροντο θείοις
πνεύμασι κλώστηρα μόρω κρεκοίσαι
ὠς χρόνω χόρδας ἔπος αἶι ψάλλει
μάτερος ἦδυ.

εἶεν, ἠρώτησέ με Ἀφρόδιτα,
νῦν ἄκουεις; ναὶ, ἐλέγην, ἄκουω.
μειδίαμά δ' ἀθανάτῳ προσώπῳ
ἄκρον ἴδοιμι.

Notes
Meter: Sapphic Stanzas
– ^ – × | – ^ ^ – | ^ – ×
– ^ – × | – ^ ^ – | ^ – ×
– ^ – × | – ^ ^ – | ^ – ×
– ^ ^ – ×

1 βίω = βίου (masc. gen. sg.)
2 ὠράνῳ = ουράνῳ
3 κύκλοισι = κύκλουσι (3pl. pres. ind. act. – ουσι(ν) → -οισι(ν))
4 ἄρχαν = ἄρχων (fem. gen. pl.)
5 κὰτ = κατά
6 Περσέφονας = Περσεφόνης (fem. gen. sg.)
7 τῶ θανάτω = τοῦ θανάτου (masc. gen. sg.)
10 μόρω = μόρου (masc. gen. sg.)
κρεκοίσαι = κρεκούσαι (fem. pres. act. part. – ουσα → -οισα)
11 χρόνω = χρόνου (masc. gen. sg.)
αἶι = ἀεί
12 μάτερος = μήτερος
13 Ἀφρόδιτα = Ἀφροδίτη (nom/voc.)

Translation: *Song*

Now listen, she said, to the song of life:
Bright stars in the broad sky wheel
Telling the story of endings
and beginnings.

The black earth each year sings
Persephone's homecoming in spring with
Different colors and the coldness of death
When she leaves again.

The voices of mortals are carried by divine
Breaths weaving the thread of fate
Just as the sweet voice of a mother always
Plucks the chords of time.

Well then, Aphrodite asked me, now
Are you listening? Yes, I said, I am listening.
And I might have seen the corner of a smile
On her deathless face.

## *Blue Bird*

Like a blue bird I take flight
and soar up into the Night
my wings beat a steady song
that can be heard all night long.

Fly with me and you will see
From the mountains to the sea.
Don't fret if you grow weary
We can perch on any tree.

A warning I must impart:
If we find ourselves apart
Do not try to cage me in,
For like a bird I will dart.

*Stone-Carved*

I see her dancing lithely from afar,
a girl with limbs so pale and fair,
no stain could mar
her skin so pure, her curling hair,
of marble white did seem just like a star.
But never shall I see her dancing here,
nor hear her voice in song:
the centuries long
have borne aloft the girl just like a stone-carved bier.

## *A Ballad of Maidenhood*

While picking flowers with my friend
enjoying Spring amid the field
our wedding day we'd play pretend
with flower rings our vows we sealed
our cowbells virgin ballads pealed
an omen soon it came to show
when told our oath to never yield
my mother asked me did I know?

That day my maidenhood did end
to virgin huntress I appealed
no god did come my case defend
So vows of union marriage sealed
and bells the wedding ballads pealed
his wagon filled with seeds to sow
then deed of love afore concealed
my husband asked me did I know?

Like shades from Hades' gloom ascend
the wagon back to mother wheeled
just as a babe when arms extend
upon her lap in tears I kneeled
embracing me our sorrows healed
and that her love would never go
as long as stars above us wheeled
my mother asked me did I know?

So Death in hand his scythe to wield
in fields of Spring where flowers grow
a truth of Nature's seed revealed
the goddess asked me did I know?

*An Ode to Earth, Mother of All*

From chaos born amid the starless sky
the goddess Gaia bare and young as day
whose power none may easily defy
where mortal men were molded from her clay.
Adorned in silky threads of blue and green
her wide horizon cradles all with breath
while down below her skirts dwell souls unseen
for Mother Earth commands both life and death.
When comes the day my soul departs from me
to caverns black and gloomy as a tomb,
then bury me beneath a shady tree,
and send my body back to earthly womb.
As mother's bosom fed my growing bones,
in death shall Gaia feed me to the stones.

# DEATH

*Fragmentary Night*

And here we are,
at the night's feverish height,
alone.

*The Descent of Aeneas*

Golden bough on Elm of Dreams
Falsely sent by iv'ry means.
If the dead can claim its coin,
May he cross the Acheron.
But if the living choose to stay,
Never will they see the day.

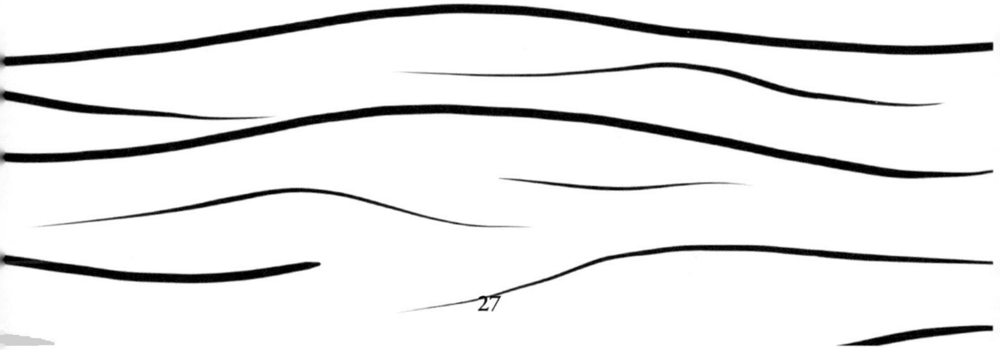

*Red Star*

In the sky late at night can be seen a red star,
Like a flame in the dark he burns hot with desire,
For the beauty of Venus so close yet so far,
While her husband Hephaestus beholds them in ire.

"In my bed I await you," said Venus to Mars,
So he silently came to her after the night
Pulling taut the day's blanket across all the stars
To rekindle their love while they hid in plain sight.

When Hephaestus left Venus and rode far away,
All alone sat the goddess in bed with a blush,
Then in secret he came and in love spent the day,
Their fair limbs all entangled and cheeks hot with flush.

But in guile had her husband set ropes in her bed,
In the act he entrapped them for gods all to see,
In their shame still embracing their faces bright red,
By his skill no brute strength could the ropes ever flee.

In the gathering crowds all the gods saw and mocked,
Yet when asked if he'd bear such a shame just for love,
The god Hermes said, "Wrap me in chains thrice as locked,
Still I'd sleep with the goddess as all watched above."

But Poseidon in pity of Mars in such straits,
To Hephaestus he paid to redress the god's guile,
Then released from their chains those adulterous mates,
And to Paphos went Venus away with a smile.

In the watches of night the red War-God still burns,
To all lovers a witness, in spite of their crime,
A red star in the sky so long Earth always turns,
Who burns hottest for you, who will never be mine.

*Eros*

Golden youth, molten eyes flung
a vision of immortal Sun in the sky hung,
riding a white chariot across my tongue,
trembling, as if inside him a fountain of Gaia sprung,
my fingers in his curls; copper I wrung.
His sly, silent lips when kissed almost stung,
flush and brimming with blood so young:
ravish me with a siren's soft symphony sung.

*An Ode to Nausicala, Princess of Scheria*

Of fair Nausicala please sing,
O Muse, the daughter of the king,
our princess with the lovely-hair
Whose voice was heard in summer air
by fields of flowers, meadows lush,
her song as tender as a thrush,
and dancing lithe among the trees
would hum a tune just like the bees
from flowers sweet to rushing stream
her eyes like emeralds did gleam.

The jewel of King Kleomachus,
Nausicala, of her tell us,
when wandering by shores alone,
she found a man bereft of throne—
a king from distant lands had sailed,
until a storm his ship assailed.
For fond of strangers was the man,
to visit every tribe his plan;
his home he left before he wed,
against his mother's wish he fled
across the wine-dark Middle Sea.

For days he never saw a tree,
nor flower fair or meadow lush,
nor listened to a singing thrush,
until aboard his ship afar,
beneath the twinkling northern star
a rocky land seen midst the waves
where might be rivers, deer, or caves.
Then thirst and hunger found respite,
or enemies became a plight
those mortals cruel, unjust, and wild,
their temples bare and gods defiled,
upon his ships brought death and pain,
so none will there return again.

His troubles hence began anew
when wrathful winds against him blew,
his ship Poseidon drowned in ire,
alone he swam the ocean dire.

His body washed upon our shore,
where danced Nausicala before,
his heart with love did fill at sight
of princess fair who stared in fright
at princely face beneath brine hid,
though sweet his words when her he bid
to save his life from certain death.
Then stole he swift the maiden's breath,
so tenderly she washed his face
with cloth she ripped from dress of lace
and brought him back to royal hall
to supplicate the king of all.

But fury wrought the man in them
for fear that aid the gods condemn
to strangers given since the day
Odysseus there made his way.
When proud Kleomachus refused,
Nausicala her heart he bruised,
where love afore had grown between,
a curse the king had not foreseen.
In secret did his daughter plan
to sail away and save the man
from certain death away from home
or on the seas forever roam.

Her father grieved when morning came,
revenge inside his breast aflame,
bewailing loud his daughter's flight
with King Philoxenos at night.
So gathering his forces strong
he sailed to right the captor's wrong,
and after years of cities seen,
he found Nausicala the queen
in Helena, with their new king,
whose mother died alone last spring.

In fury Kleomachus fought
against the Helenes and sought
his daughter lovely-haired and fair
beleaguered with her husband there,
where children she had borne by him,
two sons who fought in battle grim.
When eldest Alexandros died,
then bitter tears in bed she cried,

but hearing of her husband's death,
Nausicala, she lost her breath,
and silently without a cry
she climbed upon the palace high
then jumped she straight into her doom
to join her love in Hades' gloom.

O woe! her father did bemoan,
And sailed to Scheria alone,
Bereft for life of daughter fair
Nausicala with lovely hair.

*To Aphrodita (Translation of Sappho's Fragment 1)*

Prism-throned immortal Aphrodita,
Deceit-dealing daughter of Zeus, I beg you,
Master me not with desire nor distress,
Mistress, nor my heart,

But come here—if ever—as once
Hearing my songs from afar
You listened, and leaving your father's house
You came yoking a golden

Chariot. Lovely sparrows led you
Swiftly over the dark earth
Whirling fast-flitting wings from heaven
In mid-air.

Quickly they came: and you, O blessed,
A smile on your deathless face
Asked what again I suffered and why
Again I called

And what I most wanted to happen
In my maddened heart: "Whom again do I persuade
To lead you back into their love? Who,
O Sappho, wounds you?

For if she flees, soon she will follow,
And if she does not allow gifts, still she will give,
And if she does not love, soon she will love,
Even unwilling."

So come to me now, loosen me from cruel
Pursuit, and whatever my heart longs
To be told, tell it, and you yourself
Be my ally.

*Hymn to Demeter (in Anglo-Saxon verse)*

The mother of maiden, she mourned for her daughter,
by fairies in fields far was taken to forests
beneath the dark depths of the earth where the dead lie,
her sorrowful dirges she sang like a spell cast
and tattered her dresses and tore up her tresses
to cover her coils she cloaked herself gray-dark
and sped across seas with her sandals so swiftly
to find her fair daughter, Persephone Korē.

She came to the kingdom of Celeus in costume
a woman at well of town waiting for water
too old to bear babes but she's able to nurse them,
to palace of princes the women all brought her,
declared herself Dos in disguise was Demeter,
then King of Eleusis elated he lodged her
to nurse his new younglings the princes of kingdom
so taught she Triptolemos tilling and plowing,
the brother of baby Demophon who burned in
the flames of the fire but his mother saw frightened.

Then goddess gave back the great gifts of the deathless
enraged she revealed her full wrath and revenge plot,
the women bowed awe-struck and worshiped the goddess
so mysteries made the dear mother departed
to find her fair daughter across the far fields but
she didn't go far when her mother flew down from
the peaks of Olympus, where Pantheon gathers,
and spoke to her daughter, Demeter the deathless,
the mountain of mothers they call goddess Rhea:

"My daughter, now cast off your veil dark and hearken
to me, my son Zeus has arranged the theft-marriage
and given the goddess Persephone dear to
the Death-god your brother by blood and by marriage
by father and ruler of all with his thunder
and lightning bolt, listen to reason and lay low
your wrath which has withered the crops of the world round
and bring back the spring to the black earth below us!"

So saying to daughter then spoke dark Demeter,
"Not now or eternity, never shall crops grow

on Earth every year lest from Death comes my daughter!"
Then sped the Grain-Goddess from Great Mother Rhea
and crying she cast herself down on a rock-bed
in mourning she moaned for her daughter's new marriage,
lamenting aloud for all gods to be witness,
when far off in fields she saw flying a figure
who Hermes in hand led from Hades below them.
Rejoicing return of her daughter she ran to
her, asking Persephone, "Answer me this, please,
did Hades come find you in fields and then take you?
And ever you ate any food of the fairies?
Now speak and don't spare me not one little detail!"

"Oh mother," said maiden now married to Death-god,
"Afar in the fields I was snatched by the fairies
and borne down below to the bane of all mortals
where souls by the shores of the Styx linger sadly
and wait for the ferryman wading the waters
then Hades to halls of his home he did bring me
in couches of cushions with careful embroidery
he slipped me in secret six seeds of the fruit that
grows red in the grove by the Acheron river
so not shall I rise from the Netherworld now but
for two-thirds of year upon Earth when the clime turns
before back below I must go to my kingdom
as Queen of the Dead, wise Persephone Death-Wife,
where reigning my realm I rule equal to Hades."

So sing I in song the sad story of maiden
Persephone, daughter of Deo, the dark-cloaked,
but soon I shall honor you singing another!

*Andromache's Dirge*

To see him standing proud upon the ramparts there,
he seemed a god with sword and shield so tall and fair,
my husband true who fought against the enemy,
so Troy from those blood-thirsty Achaeans may be set free,
to see him standing with our babe so tall and fair,
he seemed a god, with sword and shield upon the ramparts there.

*I'll Be Waiting*

Did you know over the hills,
Around the mountain,
Across the sea,
Beyond the edge of forests,
I'll be waiting for you
To come to me?

Did you know on the wind,
Along the river,
By the field,
Beside the wide blue lake,
I'm happy, free, and
Forever healed?

Did you know in the sky,
Above the clouds,
With the birds,
Among the shining stars,
I sing a song of love
Without words?

Did you know someday,
You will travel too,
Over land and sea,
Across mountains, forests, and rivers?
There I'll be waiting for you
To find me.

## *The Descent of Ištar into the Underworld*

In the days of Anu and Enlil in Nineveh, Assyria ruled
the King Ammi-Saduqa of Babylon, twenty-one years had he reigned,
in the first of the Mesopotamian dynasties, none had him fooled,
neither enemies old nor his closest of friends with their praises oft feigned.

In the Royal Library of Ashurbanipal he ordered the scribes
in clay tablets to write down the falling and rising of Ištar the Queen,
the bright star Ninsi'anna, Divine among Heaven and worshiped by tribes
across lands rich and fertile the rivers Euphrates and Tigris between.

In her quest for true knowledge the goddess traverses the Path of the Dead
to the Land where none enter may leave and return to the living again.
At the door Ištar knocked and demanded her entry to Kur, then she said:
"I will make the dead rise—who devour those alive—to exceed living men!"

Past the seven-gate palace of Ereshkigal, Queen of Death, she then strode,
Ištar's sister, her enemy, ruling in Kur on her Underworld throne,
a land barren of life, filled with dust as a river where water once flowed
but had dried up and withered the plants that around it had never more grown.

By the rules of the Underworld, ancient and cruel, at each gate must undress
till she stood before sister the Queen without clothes and demanded to know,
but the arbiter dealt to her sixty diseases to kill the goddess,
by command of her sister, Ereshkigal, Queen of the Earth down below.

At once ceased was the love between mates that must be for creation of life,
no more bulls mounted cows, no more roosters with hens, no more flowers and bees,
even man he no longer in bed laid in love and impregnated wife,
and among all the livestock and crops as in Kur flourished death and disease.

So then Ea sent down a man dazzling in beauty and feminine charm,
who enchanted the Queen to bring back goddess dead to the living again,
then above the horizon arose the Queen Ištar recovered from harm,
as the star in the sky, Ninsi'anna, at night shines above mortal men.

But the price of her life was the death of a soul to be chosen by her,
while in secret her sister commanded the husband of Ištar, Tammuz,
be perfumed and by joy-girls be cheered, so the wrath of his wife he'll incur,
and be sent down below to replace her: the sister Ereshkigal's ruse.

*Fragment 2 to Aphrodite*

Aphrodite's hot
breath, heavy and sweet, swept in
with you, as a hot
gust of wind follows a door
swung wide in the summer heat.

*Facilis Descensus Averno (a Horatian Ode)*

“Descent to Hell is easy,” said
the Sibyl. “Quick like sleep in bed.”
“I’ve done it once,” said I,
“the day he said goodbye.”

Then laughed the priestess from above:
“Nay, dear, your death was sealed with love!
For biting fruit so sweet
brought Hell for you to meet.”

I entered Hell with golden bough
as Death could never scare me now,
then Hades took my life
and asked me be his wife.

But secretly I ate the seed
and lying there I did the deed,
“I love you,” Hades said.
I laughed: “Then love is dead!”

But even down below the earth
where spirits dwell in darkling dearth,
I smelled a flower’s scent:
a sign of Spring’s advent.

Thus came the time to leave him there
and dance once more in fields so fair.
“Don’t fret!” Then Death I kissed.
“To die is easiest.”

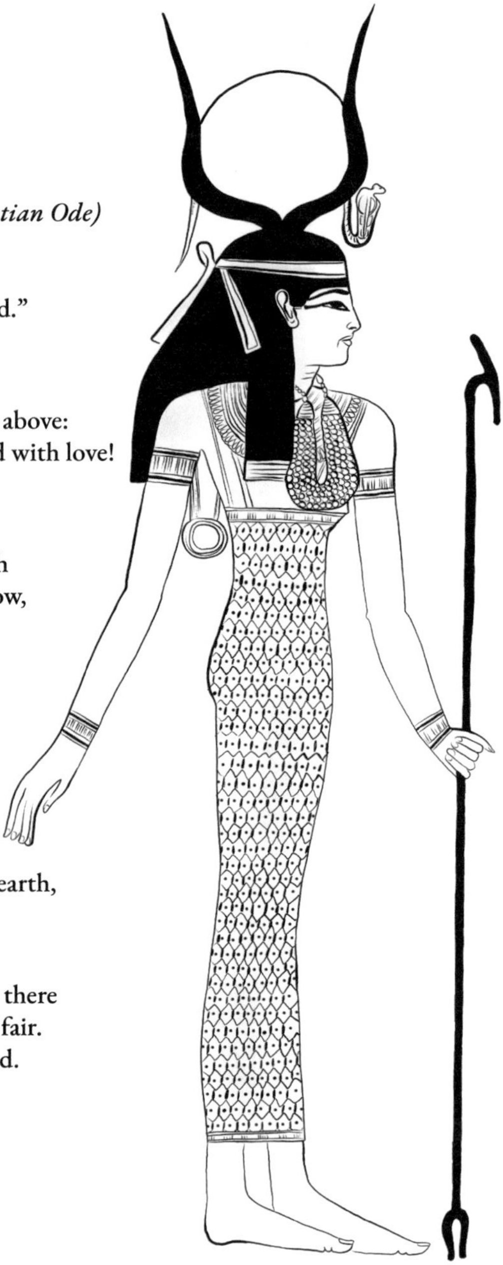

## *Hymn to Isis, Mother-Goddess*

Sing to me, Muse, of the Earth and the Mother of gods and men,
wife of Osiris and Queen of the World between sky and land,
Isis, the goddess of all and to whom I shall sing again,
healing the body of brother and husband Set slayed by hand.

Gathering all of the parts she assembled his form once more,
wrapping his limbs in white linen as once did the Kings of old,
Isis in grief rent her dress and with tears at her hair she tore,
anger at husband and brother for dying her songs all told.

Over his body the Queen said the spells old and sorcerous
blowing in breath to restore his life doomed to the world below
struck with desire she then lay with him birthing a son, Horus,
leaving her husband as King of Duat where the dead souls go.

Thus does the goddess of all ferry mortals who die like him,
husband and brother Osiris, below to where none return,
mother of Horus, protectress from evils, we sing this hymn
honoring you with our song, till we rest in our darkling urn.

*In Memoriam of my Lost Maidenhead*

Alas for Spring when flowers bloom
and fields are green in early May
the songs of birds so sweet and gay
like dirges prophesy my doom.

Alone I sit inside my room
while girls in verdant meadows play
but all I see outside is gray
as fingers nimble work the loom.

Though Spring is born by Nature's womb
still tears I cry for fated day
my maidenhead was snatched away
and carried off by loving groom.

Each year I see the flowers bloom
their saplings shoot from earthly clay
but deep inside there breeds decay
an aging corpse my girlhood's tomb.

*Fragment of a Sailor's Song*

πρὸς ζόφον ἠερόεντ᾽ ἀνέμῳ δε φέροντ᾽ ἕπευ ἄκρον
τοῦ μέσσου ἁλὸς εἶτ᾽ ἕπευ Ἠελίῳ τε δύνοντι
ἦ ἵνα ἀσφοδελὸς λειμών ἐστ᾽ ἀείμνηστος

Follow the wind as it blows West
To the edge of the Middle Sea
Then follow the Sun as it sets
To where the undying fields be...

# WISDOM

*Fragmentary Doubt*

what matters?
surely,
not you and I

*Glyphs*

Give me a sign, Venus, goddess and star so fair!
Tell me what is love if
Death bears away all those dear to below his lair,
Marked with nameless carved glyph,

Never above on this Earth to be seen again!
Show me, goddess bright, whose
Light hath for centuries shone from the sky on men,
long beheld as War's muse,

What is the meaning of life that is bound to end?
Pity mortal's bane—Death,
knowledge unknown, only after we apprehend
when we take our last breath.

*The Old Man of the Sea*

πωλεῖταί τις δεῦρο γέρων ἅλιος νημερτὴς
ἀθάνατος Πρωτεὺς πολυπλάγκτῳ ἐν νήσῳ
θηῆται ἣν ναύτης οὐ θρασὺς οὔτ' ἄναξ ἀνδρῶν
γὰρ δὲ φιλεῖ φῶκας νέποδας καλῆς ἁλοσύδνης
ἄλλα πέτηται νηῦς ἂν πνοιῇς ἀνέμοιο
παρθένος ἠΰκομος δ'ἐν νηΐ μιν οἴη θέλγει

Here haunts the Old Man of the Sea who tells no lies,
the deathless Proteus, on the Wandering Isle,
Where no brave sailor nor lord of men may see,
For only seals, daughters of Lady Brine, loves he,
But if a ship by the wind's blowing flies
Only a lovely-haired maiden aboard will him beguile.

*Bones of the Homeric Dialect*

I

To the grammar rules hearken and learn like schoolboys
the old monk's most beloved teen torturing tactic
first your the's they make ὁ's while the plural takes οἱ's—
I apologize now if I'm sounding didactic
even syntax and grammar can turn good ole Troy's
ten-year-long Trojan War a bit anticlimactic—
Oh hi hey! For the girls, it's a ἡ, neuter τό.
Oh hey hi! In the plurals, there's αἱ, τὰ—too slow?

II

Make it quick! and recite your alpha and beta,
gamma theta both rhyme but not iph you say phi,
If you hey! then that's breathing a rough on eta,
next is delta and omicron, math likes the pi,
kappa's kay and lambda l, in last is zeta.
But nu! Wait, I mean no! 'Cause there's mu, tau, and chi,
but that's x, not a xi, and then rho, epsilon,
u goes last—no, not you—then we end upsilon!

III

"That's an oopsss! Like the psssi, which you failed to mentionsss,"
sigma hissed, but what's missing I'd no iota.
Now recite without missing those noun declensions:
first, there's first and then second, and third is last—ah!
I must hurry! the teacher will give detentions!
O is anyone's game but feminine's alpha,
both in -ης and in -ας for the masculine nouns,
well, well, learning your Greek's not as fun as it sounds!

IV

Oh no, sounds are so simple, just wait for the numbers:
one is εἷς but then ask your friend Homer it's ἴα,
δύο, τρία will put all the kids into slumbers,

four is *πίσυρες*, but don't confuse *τέσσαρα*,
it's Homeric whose dialect often encumbers
like the cities and Zeus, even ships like *νῆα*
also *νῆυς* and *νέα* and more than *νέες*,
frankly spelling in Homer is quite a big mess!

V

For your pronouns I fear that it only gets worse
I is μευ and εμέο, εμέθεν as well
and that's just in possessive of Homeric verse
not to mention first plural, and second is hell,
while the third is unfortunately as diverse
with fourteen different ones 'cause the spelling's pell-mell,
but the worst of them all are the verbs, they're up next,
so be careful with endings; they're fairly complex!

VI

To dear Homer the augment is often passé,
while the passive and middle can look all brand new,
for the third: the two endings are both he and they,
for the second in singular four ends for 'you',
while short vow'ls in subjunctive may lead you astray,
thank infinitive endings they just come in two.
To conclude please take particles pinched with your salt,
when the meter is off he inserts *δέ* to halt.

VII

So the grammar rules listed may make you feel grim
when you follow Achilles to Troy's city walls,
and you mix the word 'ship' with both 'temple' and 'swim,'
and you missed the augment for when Patrocles falls,
and the wrath that came next of which sings the famed hymn,
in a dead ancient language none living recalls.
As the scholars who dig up old bones from yond times,
we find Homer's old dialect buried in rhymes.

*The Golden Shuttle*

The Golden Shuttle wove in dread
all fates of mortals trapped by thread
like flies in spider's net ensnared
no soul once caught in web be spared.

By Morai spun the threads of Fate
allotted each on loom a weight
and woven back and forth by one
thus may the will of Zeus be done.

Until the last with hated shear
when curséd day of death draws near
the thread of life untimely snipped
not when nor how may man predict.

So weaves the Golden Shuttle still
up till the loom divine they fill
whose cloth shall godly halls adorn
when all the cosmos be reborn.

*Isidorē's Hymn*

Isidorē by the village of Narmuthis,
South on the edge of the Fayyum Oasis'
Temple he carved in the stone wall his hymns to Her,
Goddess of All, through the sky the first voyageur,
Ordering Sun and the Moon and the Stars above,
Separator of the heavens and earth whereof,
Man in his folly she teaches her Ways to him,
Just as did Isidorē in his sacred hymn,
Sing to her, Isis of Egypt and Earth-Mother,
Promising later to sing to her another.

*In My Library*

Tall and lofty are their heights,
Wide and vast as the sea,
Filled with wings as pale as doves,
Softly sawed from a tree.

Draped in cloths of purple and red,
Like an emperor crowned to be,
But inside each lies a magic door,
That cannot be opened with a key.

Only silence unlocks the pages,
Letting the words inside free,
But my soul flies to distant lands,
as I read in my library.

## *Hymn to Amphitrite*

The Nereids on Naxos danced
when King of Ocean there advanced
among the lovely nymphs who twirled
with liquid feet, their braids unfurled,
and saw the august, ox-eyed maid,
fair Amphitrite, whom he bade
to run away as lovers do,
so wedding wreath to him she threw.

Now down in ocean's deep they dwell
unless you heed the tales they tell
on Naxos heavenly they say
when Lord Poseidon came that day
how Nereus' daughter fled
to mountains tall where none dare tread,
the Titan pillars of the sea,
where virgin still she might roam free.

For long he sought her far and wide
so King might have his ocean bride
and sent out creatures everywhere
to lure the nymph back to his lair,
but one by one returned alone
and wept the King atop his throne
until one dolphin swam the seas
and found her hid by Titan's knees.

Then pleaded long for her return
and not Poseidon's love to spurn.
Endeared by thoughts of lover dear,
on Delphin's back as steed to steer
she swiftly rode to Ocean's floor
where shiny shells and pearls they wore.
In golden palace ruled the King,
Poseidon, Dark-Haired, Earth-Quaking.

His trident gold commands the sea
for none there be so strong as he.
To kingly throne did dolphin swim,
then Amphitrite sat by him,
the Queen of Aegae, fish and seals,

of dolphins, whales, sting rays, and eels,
who rules the moaning breakers loud
on open sea where fishes crowd.

The eldest Nereid of all,
with august, ox-eyes did enthrall
Poseidon, Shaker of the Earth,
whom Tritan by his wife gave birth.
To honor Delphin, Lord of Steeds,
immortalizing his good deeds,
the King of Ocean raised him high
and cast the daemon in the sky.

There now Delphinus shines so bright,
his stars like shells and pearls gleam white,
reflected in the wine-dark sea,
when summer skies from winter flee,
before he dives beyond the edge
as once he swam to rocky ledge,
the Atlas Mountains, Titan's bane,
where by his knees the nymph had lain.

Fulfilling Lord's behest he bore
the maid, as wife forever more
of Ocean, Earth-encircling,
now Queen beside Olympian King,
a marriage born among the waves
where ill-lucked sailors find their graves.

*Faith*

If I could see a
sky full of stars I think I'd
believe in the gods.

*Circe*

A goddess mortal men desire
who sings while weaving by the fire
with voice as sweet as honeyed wine
by wand her spells turn men to swine.

But lucky shall the sailor be
who eats the herb gods call *moly*
a flower white whose roots are black
protecting him from her attack.

By threatening her with his knife
then swiftly shall she plead for life
and in her bed bedecked in fur
she'll ask the man to lie with her:

the goddess, Circe, lovely-tressed
whose purple robes he now undressed.
For neither drug nor spell beguiles
so dangerously as woman's wiles.

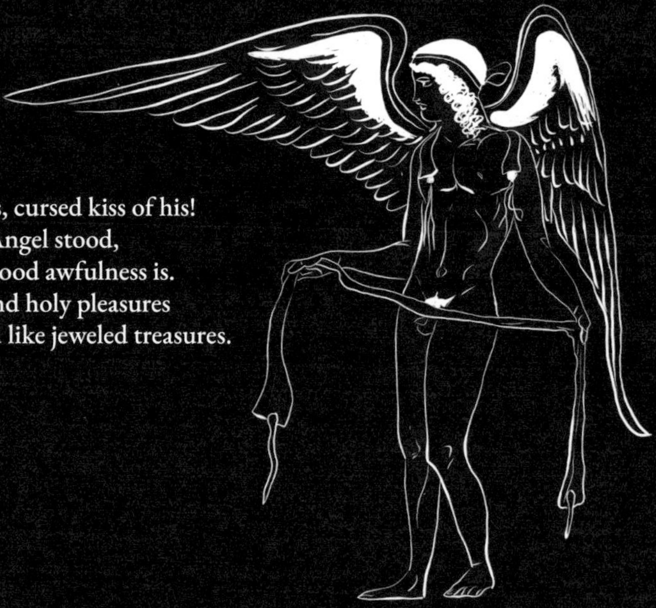

*The Fall*

Cursed fingers, cursed kiss of his!
Abashed the Angel stood,
and felt how good awfulness is.
Sick prayers and holy pleasures
scatter the bed like jeweled treasures.

*Livia, the Mermaid*

Beware the seas, said captain old,
to handsome Prince a tale he told
of monsters dread beneath the deep
where siren songs send men to sleep
but worst of all by far is she
the princess of the Middle Sea
a mermaid graced with lovely-hair
whose deadly voice must men beware
lest hearing song so soft and sweet
will jump the sailor down to meet
the Ocean's daughter, Livia,
her crown adorned with nymphaea.

So listened Prince with fear that he
shall danger find across the sea
but soon forgot of sirens fair
or mermaids graced with lovely hair
amid the green-blue ocean waves
on isles slept the crew in caves
until a storm their ship did drown
and sunk the prince forever down
the death of such a handsome man
had Fate not held another plan
his life by mermaid fair was saved
and swam him back to shore amazed.

Upon her face his gaze then fixed
and love like flowers grew betwixt
the prince and mermaid lovely-haired
his wish to marry her declared
but King of Middle Sea forbade
the union that their love had made
commanding Prince return to land
removing ring from daughter's hand
a bitter day for Princess fair
who nearly drowned in her despair
then swore her lover as he left
one day they will not be bereft.

For months the Prince lamented loud
his severed heart by father proud

and searched for antidotes or spells
and hearkened prophecies in shells
with hopes that soon his lover fair
the mermaid with the lovely hair
will once again be his to keep
and by her bed of seaweed sleep
but none to him brought lover lest
her Father proud their union blessed
so sailed he ‘cross the Middle Sea
to set the lovely princess free.

An angry storm the King then brewed
to drown the man his daughter wooed
but midst the wrathful waves he cried
to father swore if made his bride
the Prince would leave his land behind
and to the sea his soul would bind
then Ocean calmly did agree
to set the mermaid princess free
and casting spells with trident gold
a tail of sparkling scales did mold
then merman handsome swam away
with Princess Livia that day!

So tells the captain old and gray,
when asked why Prince had sailed away,
but none believed the man survived
when drowning had then been revived
by mermaid lovely-haired and fair
nor how began their love affair
yet if you listen by the shore
you might just hear them evermore
together singing soft and sweet
a grace to sailors if they meet
upon the waves of Ocean dire
whose love betwixt shall never tire.

*Sailor's Superstition*

Black is moon to start anew,
White is moon for spells,
Gold and red is moon at sea
If soon come stormy swells.

## *A Marriage Song*

The bells! the bells they ring today
and voices loudly cheer
for loving union formed between
a man and his wife dear.

The bells! the bells of churches call
to bless the baby born
from loving union birthed a boy
on blissful yestermorn.

The bells! the bells they chime again
and voices sweetly sing
when son now grown weds lovely bride
and seals it with a ring.

The bells! the bells alas they sound
and mourners loud lament
for mother dear in death departs
to blissful heaven sent.

The bells! the bells of churches clang
and voices sing a song
for daughter born to union sweet
a gift for man lifelong.

The bells! the bells again ring clear
for father laid to rest
beside his wife their union sealed
in death as life were blest.

The bells! the bells of angels toll
and mortal choirs sing
a marriage song for newly weds
as church bells ring-a-ling!

*Sowing Seeds*

and when the world stops
turning, how do you find the
tether? the seed? the
link between one dream and the
next?

# SPRING

*Fragmentary Time*

time has shifted in
its imperceptible way
to a new dimension
in me

*Spring Again*

It's Spring again and Earth delights anew
when Mother reunites with Daughter dear
and tears of separation dry like dew
as Dawn unfurls and flowers grow in fields
where once a maiden fair was snatched by Death
returned to Life when Winter melts away.

Arise and 'ere the break of day away!
Amid the woods and dells sing birds anew
like Phoenixes reborn from ash in Death
and mother-bears emerge with younglings dear
while wolves and deer alike now prance in fields
where flower petals bead with morning dew.

From leaf and blade of grass the sun melts dew
and chases wintry winds and frost away
so green may grow once more in flower fields
and rose and narcissus may sprout anew
which maidens near to wedding day hold dear
remembering Persephone and Death.

In fields the maidens sing a song of Death
their dancing lithe and voices soft as dew
for soon shall mother whom they hold most dear
be left behind when wed and ride away
for man and woman joined start life anew
and build a home in far off fertile fields.

Then comes the Winter burying the fields
where snow and frost bring flowers fair to Death
and wintry winds kill crops and cows anew
and breath of chilly Dawn makes frost from dew
when Hades bears the maiden fair away
and cloaked Demeter grieves her daughter dear.

Alas! how daughter ran to mother dear
as flowers bloom like rainbows in the fields
and grief like frost the sunlight chased away
but tricked to eat six seeds in bed by Death
Persephone bewailed with tears like dew
for now must maiden fair descend anew.

It's Spring again when wife so dear to Death
returns to fields above now kissed with dew
while far away they sing this song anew.

*Flowers Bloom*

The difference between weeds and flowers
Lies in how they grow,
While weeds greedily claw at the sky,
Flowers they bloom slow.

This difference between weeds and flowers,
might not matter much,
yet the one chokes beauty from the ground,
one we crave to touch.

While the weed works more efficiently,
flowers take their time:
For I always found the hours worth wasting,
making poems rhyme.

*The Mountains by the Sea (A Villanelle)*

O mountains by the sea
whom earth and water bore
how dear you are to me.

Adorned with rock and tree
whose feet kiss sandy shore
O mountains by the sea.

Where Nature can run free
as birds near treetops soar
how dear you are to me.

How much I shall miss thee
when one day I'm no more
O mountains by the sea.

I'll never tire to see
green hillsides ebb ashore
how dear you are to me.

As lovely as can be
who stand forever more
O mountains by the sea
how dear you are to me.

*Marriage Bed*

In rocky Ithaca she stayed,
Her husband by the gods delayed,
By day she wove in silent dread,
Of suitors cruel in her halls fed,
To stall their greedy appetite,
Unraveled in deceit by night,
A shroud for poor old Laërtes,
His son still lost to wine-dark seas.

For twenty years his labors long,
Immortalized in Homer's song,
Kept far the arms of loving wife
and tossed about the waves in Strife,
Odysseus who sailed the sea
and longed for dear Penelope
but by Poseidon's wrath invoked
his Fate bound tight as oxen's yoke.

Across the ocean wide to roam
the hero must to come back home
but sirens, beasts, and Cyclopes
enough to shake a soldier's knees
he fought and lost his comrades dear
but never lost himself to fear
and goddesses both cunningly
entrapped on isles enchanting he
whom nymph Calypso, Circe fair
for eight long years held captive there.

When gods immortal him returned
the Argive hero homeward yearned
and after greedy suitors killed
their blood in homely halls he spilled.
Then asked his wife a question sly
to move their bed but in reply
her husband swore no god could move
their marriage bed and so did prove
his love like roots of tree trunk deep
where bed he carved for them to sleep
and so she led him to their room
like once they did as bride and groom.

*An Ode to Orion*

Bejeweled and armored belt and bow,
A hunter poised to shoot,
He arcs across wide-skirted Night,
His twanging arrow mute.

Pursuing Dawn her early light,
Eternal lovers cold,
By Artemis the giant slain,
A hero famed of old.

But some another tale they tell,
Of how the huntsman died,
When Gaia sent the Scorpion,
To quench his raging Pride.

Poseidon's son succumbed to death,
For gods a bitter woe,
From pity Zeus in heaven raised,
The hunter, belt and bow.

So hero proud his stars aligned,
In winter hunts the beast,
Across was Scorpion arranged,
In summer rises east.

Thus never shall the giant slay,
Another monster bold,
The tale as ancient as the stars,
A fate the gods uphold.

## *Hymn to Persephone, Death-Bringer*

In woods of woe walks wife of Death
who bears a bough between her hands
a golden gift for grieving souls
to cross the currents cold to lands
where dead are doomed to darkling days
and light is left with living men
to speak with sorrowed souls deceased
then swift return to sun again.

Forever famed for frightening feat
of walking where the dead ones dwell
and facing fearful Hades' wife
Persephone, the Queen of Hell,
in woods of woe by waters dread,
the river Styx that shuttles souls,
and ever near the elm of dreams
by poplar trees she singing strolls
at western edge of evergreens
how husband hers in girlhood seized
like flowers fair in field afar
bewailing mother thence bereaved
who scouring skies and seas alike
lamented loud her lovely child
untimely took in maidenhood
who Hades in his halls beguiled
six pomegranate seeds he sowed
and tricked to tarry timelessly
in marriage bed below the earth
and crowned her ruler rightfully.

As dame of Death she doomed to die
all mortals in her kingdom cold
within her husband's hallowed halls
her beauty awful to behold
but Hermes herald of the gods
came quickly down to chambers kept
where Queen Persephone reclined
beside the King in bed they slept
and woke when Argus-Slayer spoke
he bade her back to mother fly

but in her arms told all the tale
then mother mourned and gave a cry
just as her daughter did that day
whom Hades bore in haste below
now down in darkness doomed to dwell
till Winter wanes and melts like snow
the grief of goddess Golden-Blade
as mother meets with daughter dear
the fate of fair Persephone
to see the sky two-thirds of year.

Then flowers bloom in fields afar
where once she walked a maiden still
before the Spring burns under sun
and colors trees with coming chill
Demeter Dark destroys the crops
in mourning stolen maidenhood
of daughter fair in flower fields
when near the narcissus she stood
and grasping it then gaped the earth
from crevice burst his chariot
her cry against the king of all
to Father Zeus whose will was wrought
he promised dear Persephone
as bride for brother Death in Hell
with equal share of sovereign
of those that move below and dwell
in darkest depths of worldly woe.

So sang the voice of Death-Bringer,
the wise Persephone, in woods
lamenting loud the loss of her
dear maidenhood and mother far
a song for woman's wedding day
when homeward husband's wagon flies
and mother's daughter moves away.

*Philo-Sofia*

Is it a coincidence
that love is a man,
truth a woman, and beauty
a cold terror in the night?

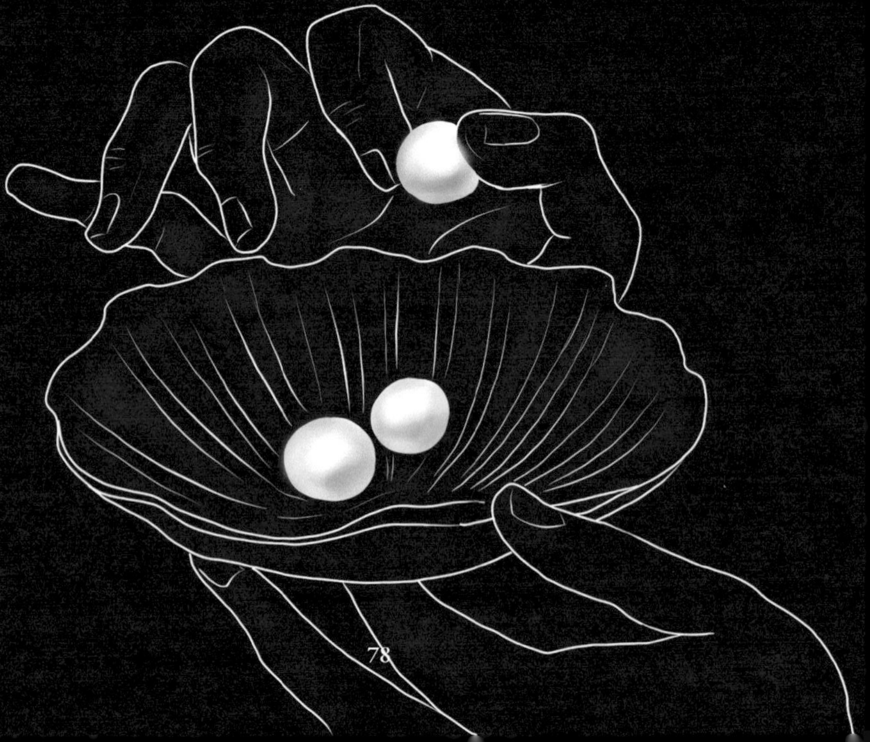

## *Pearl*

### I

Pearl I was named, princess of maids,
For lithe my limbs, lovely my locks,
Ringlets in white ribbon tied braids,
As violins so sweet my vox,
Delight in dance, my dress cascades
Like water weaves through white-foamed rocks.
They ask which eternal god aids
A maiden mere, though modest walks,
For beauty's blooming blush soon mocks
When satin pearl-white skin is stained,
Frail and faded beneath my frocks,
Gone was the Pearl, my girlhood waned.

Now younger years have gone yonder
Days of dancing, my girlhood's Dawn,
Flower fields my feet did wander
Like a maddened, maidenly faun
Sun and stars and sky to ponder
My limbs light, lithe as a swan,
When Time was tiresome to squander,
The hours unseen went on and on
So delicate they deemed me drawn
As pearls are precious, pale and pure
In oyster shells their seedlings spawn
But once obtained, gone their allure.

Suddenly slipped my pearl, gone swift
From my palm, O pitiful day!
As light as wings my legs did lift,
Flitting to and fro in fields gay,
When I chanced on a childish gift—
Narcissus—in naivete
I plucked the ploy, pleasure I sniffed,
Behold! A trick hid the bouquet,
Rapt by him, we rode far away
Down to darkness, Death's abode,
Leaving the light, I loathed the way
Gone was my pearl on gloomy road.

From mother gone her maiden dear,
A cry was caught on chilly breeze,

And lost the pearl in grassy mere,
Seized swiftly over endless seas.
We came to caverns cold and drear
Where dead dwell, dolor and disease,
No sun shone this sorrowful bier,
No precious pearls do the dead please,
No flowers fair, no flitting bees,
Save asphodels, their ageless field,
No flower, nothing will appease
Those doomed to die, the door is sealed.

II

My Fate was sealed, forgotten there,
Just as my pearl from my palm fell,
Slipped through a rift, the soil bare,
A hallowed grave, the halls of Hell,
Where lay my lover in his lair.
As pearls sit in their oyster shell,
Ever inside their lips ensnare,
In such darkling depths did I dwell,
Too many terrors there to tell,
There I had roamed from room to room,
A pearl inside a prison cell,
Sealed inside my shadowy tomb.

Our vows we sealed, my veil dark-gray,
A marriage match twixt Death and maid,
Bride and bridegroom, in bed we lay.
My husband smiled. "Come here," he bade,
"Swallow these seeds, your sorrow allay,
To eat this fruit, I once forbade,
Wisdom it holds and shows the way
Your frail mortality to fade
And the Deathless doors to invade."
Then Hades handed me the seeds,
Six pomegranate pearls to aid,
My Fate sealed shut with sinful deeds.

Our kisses sealed us Queen and King,
Holding dominion down below,
The Land of the Dead, none living,
Where the streams of dreaded Styx flow.
"Guess what of this realm by that ring
Is yours now?" he asked. "I don't know,"

I answered. He said: "Everything."
Thus bridal price he did bestow,
In payment for my pearl of woe,
Lost from me in a different life,
The cost of his tender kiss—lo!
Wisdom has sealed me as his wife.

Sealed is my soul, sovereign cold,
Promised to wed the Lord of wights,
Snatched untimely, under the wold,
Bound to darkness and bitter nights,
A misery to mother old,
Who still watches from worldly heights,
As shepherd's sheep lost from the fold,
Prays for Pearl to be in her sights.
As winter comes and the wind bites,
She lays down where her Pearl was left,
Asleep she dreams of ancient rites,
And beholds her Pearl long bereft.

## III

"Daughter bereft! Is this a bane
Or do you live, lithe and lovely?
Who stole my Pearl, bringer of pain?
Who seized you, over land and sea?
Over whose realm do you now reign?"
So she cried loud, her questing plea.
"Fast asleep you are, but no feign
Is this vision sweet—verily,
For the Lord of Death has doomed me
To reign over his barren realm,
Queen of Hell, no flower or tree
Exists, life-bereft, save this Elm:

"Sight of your bereft Pearl's shade sends
The ancient Elm, to grief allay,
The rage inside that your heart rends,
As low on the dark earth you lay—
Beware! No prayer baleful death ends,
For eaten once food of the fey
Dooms to a fate that no drug mends,
Six seeds to seal on wedding day
To immortality the way,
He showed me how, my spirit save,

His price paid for my pearl turned gray,
Bereft from me in buried grave."

Her mother stared, bereft of speech,
At queenly daughter's pearl-white dress,
Her form so tall as trees of beech
But when she wished her Pearl caress,
Arms outstretched, not able to reach,
Nor as with babes to her breast press,
For living dreams may not Death breach,
Lest the laws of loathed Hell digress.
"Cruel Death," her mother did confess,
"Who seized my daughter, doomed to die,
No pity for my Pearl's duress,
Nor mother bereft. Tell me, why?"

"Bereft? Nay, the King does not kill,
But welcomes all the wights of earth,
For Death is Life's doom by God's will,
Gifted to each mortal, so made at birth,
And all living things, loch or hill,
Must still one day be brought to dearth.
Mother, do not think of me ill!
In life there is left for you mirth,
Far more precious than pearls are worth,
Even ones left by the wayside.
Ample fruits does Ocean unearth:
Pearls spring from their shells inside."

IV

Then mother did spring from soil bare,
Tears wet her cheeks, terrible sore,
To see her Pearl, perfectly fair,
Bound to baleful death evermore,
Her hallowed face, ringlets in hair,
The gray-dark veil for bridegroom wore,
Her body lithe, her beauty rare,
Just like pearls from pale oysters tore,
Their shells washed on a far-off shore.
But in despair shall daylight dawn,
As gems are hid in jagged ore,
Spring shall come soon as winter's gone.

From green fields spring blooming flowers,

Their petals white as my pearl once shone,
Laid low in my last earthly hours,
Beside my body ground to bone,
Where grass has grown from May showers,
Hiding my grave, now mossy stone,
For reign this realm older powers
To all others their names unknown,
The seeds of life, in secret sown,
Buried in earth as pearl bereft,
Wrinkled and gray as a wise crone,
Like a spring whose water long left.

From winter spring the seeds of life,
When Mother saw a marvel made,
Her dear Pearl, doomed as Death's wife,
In fleshly raiment, fair arrayed,
Her voice as sweet as vibrant fife,
In fields of flowers danced the maid,
As once in Spring before her strife.
At awesome sight she was afraid,
Till holding Pearl did arms persuade,
Imbued with immortality,
Her purity never decayed:

Spring, as her pearl, shall always be.
Spring is the season of the bride,
Since Pearl was lost, lovely and lithe,
And in Death's dark dwelling abide,
By the hated Styx, Charon's hythe,
And the ageless Asphodel fields wide,
Where wraiths reside, bemoan and writhe,
And Death's hunting rout oft did ride,
His blowing horn resounding blithe,
And saddled near, in hand a scythe,
The Queen of Death, her kingdom famed,
Our tortured mortal souls her tithe,
Like the maid, Pearl, our poem named.

*P(s)alms*

I face my palms    to God above,
and pray to Him    my fears abate,
along this path    alone I tread,
a lonely dirge    I sing my psalms,
to heavens broad    the cloudless sky,
where angels dwell    their wings divine,
on Earth I'm bound    till day of death,
to watch the skies    where omens fly,
on palms I read    old prophecies,
of what and where    and how and when,
but never why    their runes are mute,
to answer prayers    the mortal bane,
of why this World    did come to be,
nor why I ask    why must I know,
the need of Man    he stands alone,
he looks on high    beholds the stars,
he wonders why    he prays to God,
he sings his psalms    he breaks his bread,
he tills the fields    he labors long,
then dreams at night    when Earth is dark,
of stars above,    their message cold,
and rises morn    to start the day,
when singing birds    awake to Dawn,
a song I strum    on lyre strings,
the psalm of man    he prays to God
to walk along    the path he treads
in Shadow of    the Vale of Death.

## *White Star*

In the sky near the Sun shining like a white star
reappearing at Dawn's early light and day's end
he's more clever and witty than others by far
and to mortals on Earth has been always a friend.

By the road he protects weary travelers home
nor forsaken are merchants who trade 'cross the sea
for with swift winged sandals the earth does he roam
the one god who can step over Death's boundary.

He's a helper to thieves, since from Phoebus he stole
the first day he was born his own brother he tricked
leading backward his cows from the fields where they stroll
right from under his nose the poor cattle he nicked.

In a rage did Apollo discover the theft
but asleep was the culprit, a babe in his crib,
with an innocent yawn that no one would suspect
if not stains from a roast had been seen on his bib.

Then the god gave a laugh and the baby he raised
who then showed him the lyre he'd made from a shell
of a tortoise, then singing the gods were all praised,
the creation of Gaia, how Titan gods fell.

Even told he the story of how he was born
when fair Maia with Zeus lied in love in a cave
and all deeds he himself had accomplished that morn
then to Phoebus in payment his lyre he gave.

They say Hermes will come on the day that you die
and your soul he will guide to the caverns below
where beneath the gray gloom Fields of Asphodel lie,
the white star in the sky: his swift feet all aglow.

Yet philosophers wandering Egypt's gold sand
by the teachings of Hermes shall God understand.

## *The Cosmic Question*

If I could reach up to the stars
And dip my hands in Milky Ways,
Maybe I would not feel so lost,
Like changing winds on winter days.
If I could search the underground
And dig up Earth's carved memory,
Then maybe I could understand,
How this universe came to be.
If I could hear the old trees speak,
And learn their whispered languages,
Then maybe my many regrets,
Would not seem disadvantages.
But perhaps what I'm searching for,
I cannot touch or hear or see:
All the answers to my questions
Might simply lie inside of me.

*Revelation*

Yet were all the world
coming to an end in flames
still it would be fair
to stand beneath the sun and
hear the birds sing: Nature's song.

## *An Epithalamium*

A song for bride and groom we sing!
O Hymen honor them in bed!
As marriage bells so loudly ring
a song for bride and groom we sing
and pray the gods their blessings bring
to those whom Love today has wed!
A song for bride and groom we sing!
O Hymen honor them in bed!

Today the bliss of Love draws near
between a man and his wife dear!
There stands the bridegroom tall and proud
as marriage songs are sung aloud,
like heroes tall and strong of old
with handsome face and heart so bold—
Behold! the bride is no less fair
a nymph-like smile and braided hair
beneath her yellow bridal veil
her cheeks a-flush, so lovely pale
as rays upon a flower shine
its petals soft as wings divine
of Eros flying down on high
and with his bow his arrows fly!

A song for bride and groom we sing!
O Hymen honor them in bed!
As seeds upon the couple fling
a song for bride and groom we sing
as Hymen sang on lyre string
the day that Bacchus Ariadne wed:
A song for bride and groom we sing!
O Hymen honor them in bed!

His eyes alight when bride he sees
and from his arms she screaming flees
like Daphne fair from God of Sun
across the fields and vales did run
afraid to lose her maidenhood
Apollo's love she long withstood.
Just so the bride cries out in fright
and struggles him with all her might

but when he carries wife away
on blissful blessed wedding day
then never more she mourned for her
dear maidenhood, so sweet and pure,
for lay in love the bride and groom
on nuptial couch in marriage room!

A song for bride and groom we sing!
O Hymen honor them in bed!
An oath they swore with golden ring
a song for bride and groom we sing
with Hymen, godly marriage king
as Dawn shines forth in gold and red!
A song for bride and groom we sing!
O Hymen honor them in bed!

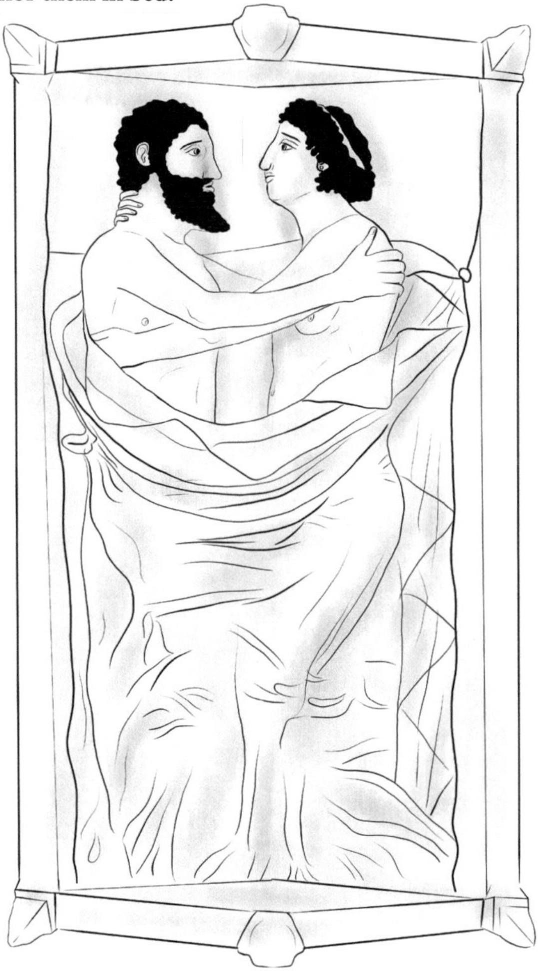

Κόρη Κόσμου *(Kore Kosmou), or The Maiden of the Cosmos*

Then God commanded, "Nature, awaken!"
and from his Word the cosmos birthed Korē,
in shape the first divinely feminine,
a maiden fair and young as dawn of day,
whose beauty all the gods beheld in awe
while stood before eternal pantheon,
her power ruled by perfect cosmic law
where Breath of God and Conscious Fire spawn.
Once Toil in the bed of Nature laid,
their daughter fair, Invention, then she bore,
who governed over all that had been made,
bestowed God's gift of being ever more.
Her Matter made He filled with Mystery
so as above then so below shall be.

# APPENDIX
## ON METER & RHYME

For those interested, I provide here a comprehensive view of the various kinds of metrical and rhyming schemes I used throughout this collection of poems, and the ways in which my poems follow—or break—convention.

## *The Nature of Meter*

For most of human history, poetry was sung or chanted orally. In fact, the distinctions between song, poetry, and story would not have been so clear in the past as they are today, so it might make more sense to think of poetry as song, which, when sung to praise or entreat a divine figure, may be called prayer. Meter, in this light, is a structured form of *rhythm*, usually natural to the language performing the song.

Different languages constructed different meters or sometimes employed borrowed metrical traditions, as Latin did with the Ancient Greek hexameter. In English verse, accentual meter arises most naturally, such as the kind we find in Old Norse, Anglo-Saxon, and Middle English poetry, one of the most famous being the Anglo-Saxon poem *Beowulf*. In accentual verse, syllables may change freely so long as the accent scheme remains the same. Take these lines from *Beowulf*:

wæs se grimma gæst     Grendel haten
mære mearcstapa     se þe moras heold

*the grim spirit     was called Grendel*
*mighty murk-stepper     he held the moors*

Despite a different syllable count, you get four stressed syllables in each line, which I have indicated below with stress marks ( ′ ) and bolded syllables:

wæs se **grim**ma **gæ**st     **Gren**del **hat**en

**mæ**re **mearc**stapa     se þe **mor**as **heo**ld

In other languages, like Spanish, French, Turkish, and Japanese, to name just a few, their meter is counted purely by syllables with no regular stress count. So we get the very well-known Japanese *haiku* with the syllable count 5-7-5, which we see in my poem *Faith*, as well as the *tanka*, which adds two more heptasyllabic lines to the *haiku*, as in my poems *Fragment 2 to Aphrodite* and *Revelation*. Playing with expected syllable counts and lines can even mirror meaning, as in my poem *Sowing Seeds*, which carries a one-syllable word onto an invented sixth line, symbolically 'linking' the phrases '*one dream*' and '*the next?*' which the poem demands to know.

In languages like Ancient Greek and Latin, however, meter depended upon syllable *weight*, not accent or number. A syllable could be heavy or light depending on a number of factors, and which determines how long or short the syllable is sung.

In the dactylic hexameter, the meter used in Homer's *Iliad* and *Odyssey*, a metrical 'foot' (or the basic metrical unit) is made up either of long-short-short (— ᴗ ᴗ) syllables, called dactyls (so named from the Greek word for 'finger,' *daktulos*, because it's made up of a long bone and two shorter ones) with a *dum-di-di* rhythm, or long-long (— —) syllables, called spondees, with a slower *dum-dum* rhythm. A single line consisted of six 'feet,' either dactylic or spondaic. If we scan the first line of the *Odyssey*, we see the following metrical scansion, with vertical lines marking the feet (which paid no attention to word boundaries):

— ᴗ ᴗ | — ᴗ ᴗ | — ᴗ ᴗ | — ᴗ ᴗ | — ᴗ ᴗ | — —
ἄνδρα μοι | ἔννεπε, | μοῦσα, πο|λύτροπον, | ὃς μάλα | πολλὰ
*ándra moi / énnepe, / moûsa, po/lútropon, / hòs mála / pollà*
"Tell me, Muse, of the man of many turns, who very much..."

Two of my poems, which I wrote in Ancient Greek, namely *Fragment of a Sailor's Song* and *The Old Man of the Sea*, are in dactylic hexameter. Their English translations, however, could not replicate a weighted meter, instead using syllabic verse with rhyming schemes that are more natural to English. In my poem Ἀοίδη, *An Original Lyric Poem in Sapphic Greek*, I wrote specifically in the ancient Aeolic dialect and in the meter that Sappho, the famed poet of the island Lesbos who lived during the late 7th to early 6th centuries BCE, would have written in, which is structured differently from the Homeric dactylic hexameter. For further explanation of the Sapphic stanza and meter, see the notes beneath Ἀοίδη.

Although my poems are heavily inspired by the Ancient Greek and Latin oral traditions (among other ancient cultures), besides the poems mentioned above, the rest were written in English and therefore mostly followed an accentual meter natural to the language. Instead of weighted syllables, each metrical 'foot' of accentual meter contains a certain number of stressed and unstressed syllables. When the metrical foot contains one unstressed syllable ( x ) followed by a stressed syllable ( ′ ), we call it *iambic*, with a rhythm of *di-dum*. When we combine four iambic feet to form one line of poetry, we have written in *iambic tetrameter*. Take, for example, the first line of *Ode to Sofia*, which would scan thus:

x ′ | x ′ | x ′ | x ′
*I used to sleep under the stars*

If we add another foot to this line, it becomes *iambic pentameter*, another foot, *iambic hexameter*, and so on. But if we rearrange the stressed and unstressed syllables within each foot to first a stressed then an unstressed syllable ( ′ x ), that's called *trochaic*, with a rhythm of *dum-di*. If we add an unstressed syllable before the iambic foot ( x x ′ ), we get *anapestic*, or *di-di-dum*, and if we switch that around ( ′ x x ), we get *dactylic*, similar to the Homeric meter, with a rhythm of *dum-di-di*. Lastly, if the stress falls in between two unstressed syllables ( x ′ x ), then we get an *amphibrachic* meter, or *di-dum-di*, as in the Sapphic stanza, which imitates the original Ancient Greek Sapphic stanza but with accentual meter instead of weighted meter. My poem *Moonrise*, also inspired by Sappho's poetry, fittingly uses the English version of the Sapphic stanza.

## *Rhyming & Stanzas*

When we add rhyming or alliteration to these metrical schemes, the poem's structure can get more complicated, but at the same time, it creates a pleasant harmony to the ear. After all, both the words *rhyme* and *rhythm* come from the same Ancient Greek word *rhythmos* (ῥυθμός), meaning generally 'measured motion or time.' Rhymes can vary greatly depending on the type of poem and the whim of the poet, and can even create small puzzles linking rhymes across lines and stanzas.

Lines are grouped together to form stanzas. A stanza can then rhyme ABAB or ABCB, or form rhyming couplets like AABBCC, or envelope ABBA, or rhyme every third line, as in my poem *I'll be Waiting*. The rhymes can even be broken or maintained across stanzas, like ABAB CDCD or ABCB CDED EFGF, which can become even more complex, as we will see below. A poem can have no rhyme and simply follow an accentual or syllabic meter, as in the haikus and tankas mentioned above, or it can combine syllable counts and rhymes, like the poems *A Oliveira* and *Bluebird*, which are both heptasyllabic, and rhyme ABCB and AABB respectively, nicely fitting for their simplistic, natural themes. Or a poem can use only rhyme, as *Eros* does, where every line of the entire poem rhymes the same.

If a stanza has four lines, we call it a *quatrain*. If we take a quatrain of alternating iambic tetrameter and trimeter along with a rhyming scheme ABCB, we get the ballad stanza, as seen in many of my poems, like *Ode to Jupiter, Deus Pater, A Marriage Song*, and *An Ode to Orion*. The ballad stanza has a deceptive simplicity that can bear a weighty message in a light, sing-songy rhythm. In *Ode to Sofia*, I mixed the ballad stanza with what's called a long measure (a stanza where all four lines are iambic tetrameter, rhyming ABCB), as can be seen in the first two stanzas, where the trimeter of the ballad stanza has been bolded:

x ´ | x ´ | x ´ | x ´
*I used to sleep under the stars* [A]
**x ´ | x ´ | x ´**
*When gods kept watch at night* [B]
x ´ | x ´ | x ´ | x ´
*And Sun chased Moon across the sky* [C]
**x ´ | x ´ | x ´**
Like two love birds in flight. [B]

x ´ | x ´ | x ´ | x ´
*If then my Fate is bound to Earth* [D]
x ´ | x ´ | x ´ | x ´
*And Spring and Winter herald Death,* [E]
x ´ | x ´ | x ´ | x ´

*Why calls Eternity my name* [F]
x ´| x ´ | x ´| x ´
*An icy wind Her divine breath?* [E]

Throughout history, certain poets have become famous for the stanzas they create with distinctive rhyming and metrical schemes, usually created for a certain medium, whether it be a play, or epic poem, or a lament. Arguably thc most famous kind of poem is the Shakespearean sonnet, which combines 14 lines of iambic pentameter rhyming ABABCDCDEFEFGG, with the last two lines forming a rhyming couplet (which, when it's iambic pentameter, is also called a *heroic* couplet). Among my poems, *An Ode to Earth* and Κόρη Κόσμου *(Kore Kosmou), or The Maiden of the Cosmos*, are examples of the Shakespearean sonnet.

Rhyming couplets form the bedrock for many of my longer poems, especially those formed in iambic tetrameter, as in *An Ode to Nausicala, The Golden Shuttle, Hymn to Amphitrite, Circe, Livia the Mermaid,* and *Marriage Bed*. For all of these poems, I desired to create a more mythic feel, which the close rhythmic, almost chanting nature of the heroic couplets certainly evokes. It is also easy to find a rhythm writing in both the swift iambic tetrameter and rhyming couplets, useful for longer compositions, and makes me think that this is the most natural metrical and rhyming scheme for English. Rhyming couplets, however, can also be found in the anapestic tetrameter of *The Descent of Aeneas,* in the dactylic pentameter of *Hymn to Isis, Mother-Goddess,* and in the dactylic tetrameter of *Isidorē's Hymn*.

If we mix up the rhyming scheme of the long measure stanza (four lines of iambic tetrameter rhyming ABCB), and instead we rhyme ABBA, we call it the I*n Memoriam* stanza, after Tennyson's famous lengthy elegy *In Memoriam* [1850], which has thus caused this kind of structure to be associated with loss and lament. My poem *In Memoriam of my Lost Maidenhood* is, fittingly, made up of four *In Memoriam* stanzas. If we add a foot to make iambic pentameter lines and change the rhyme scheme to ABAB, we get the *heroic quatrain*, which I used to write the poem *Verse Translation of the Homeric Hymn to Artemis.* If a rhyming couplet is added to the heroic quatrain, the six lines are called a sestet. In the English part of my poem *The Old Man and the Sea*, I create a variation on this with an embedded rhyming couplet ABCCAB.

### *Famous Meters & Rhymes*

As we have already seen above, specific combinations of rhyming and metrical schemes become famous when used by certain poets or time periods, like the *In Memoriam* stanza or the Shakespearean sonnet. Another example includes Dante's *Divine Comedy* and Chaucer, both of whom utilized strings of chain rhymes, ABA BAB CDC DED EFE..., whose stanzas are called *terza rima*. Four of those stanzas, capped with a couplet, form the *terza rima sonnet*, which I used to write my poem *Terra Romana nella Terza Rima*. In Lord Byron's long, satirical poem *Don Juan,* he famously used the eight-line stanza called *ottava rima*, which has the specific rhyming scheme ABABABCC. I wrote *Bones of the Homeric Dialect* in a variation of the ottava rima, but instead of iambic pentameter, I chose anapestic tetrameter to give an even more exaggeratedly jerky, comedic effect.

Another kind of poem that uses terza rima but with a more complicated linking of rhymes across stanzas is the *villanelle*. This consists of 19 iambic pentameter lines, including five 3-line stanzas and a concluding quatrain. The rhyming scheme of the first stanza, $A_1BA_2$, not only rhymes the first and third lines, but in this case, they are repeated later as refrains. The poem's full rhyming scheme is: $A_1BA_2$ $abA_1$ $abA_2$ $abA_1$ $abA_2$ $abA_1A_2$, where *a* and *b* rhyme with the As and B of the first stanza but do not repeat the exact same word. As the name suggests, my poem utilizes this schema in *The Mountains by the Sea (A Villanelle)*. Despite its complex nature, as we see in my poem, the villanelle has quite a rustic quality, reflected in its name, taken from the Italian *villano*, meaning 'peasant' or 'villa.'

As I have already touched upon, poetry and song were once indistinguishable, but one need not go back as far as Ancient Greece to see this. In medieval French poetry, there were three musical poems, the so-called *formes fixes*, which were known for their refrains. One of these, the solemn *ballade*, consisted of 3 x 8 lines rhyming $ABABBCBC_1$, where the last line was used as the refrain, repeated at the end of every stanza, including the last, which formed a four-line *envoi* rhyming $BCBC_1$. My poem *A Ballad of Maidenhood* is written in iambic tetrameter and follows the *ballade* rhyming scheme, but instead of repeating the first line perfectly, I chose to adjust the refrain to reflect who was asking the question throughout the maiden's lifetime, with the first reading *'my mother asked me did I know?'* followed by her husband asking, her mother once more, then an unnamed goddess.

Another *formes fixes* verse was the *triolet*, which originally had been sung as two melodies, matching its refrains. It had no fixed meter or length, usually written in octaves, with line 1 repeated in the 4th and 7th lines and line 2 repeated as the 8th. In my poem *An Epithalamium*, which I consider a marriage song, I alternated longer, unique stanzas of iambic tetrameter in rhyming couplets (used to narrate the wedding as it is happening) with triolets in between as a kind of joyful refrain in of themselves, while still slightly changing the 3rd, 5th, and 6th lines to maintain a contrast with the refrains *within* each triolet.

The last *formes fixes* was called the *rondeau*, based on the triolet and originating from sung dance-rounds (rondels). While I did not write any poem in a strict *rondeau*, I took inspiration from its basic rhyming unit A(R)ABBAR, where R stands for the refrain, which comes from the first part of the first line, to write *Andromache's Dirge*. My poem, which is only one stanza, takes it a step further and rhymes $A_1A_2BBA_2A_1$ but repeats the end of lines $A_1$ and $A_2$ in reverse order after an enveloped couplet while changing the first half of both lines. This gave the poem (which, after all, is a dirge) at once a solemn and yet tender air that captures the love and sorrow Andromache feels in the poem, looking at her husband, Hector, holding their babe on the walls of Troy before he returns to battle.

I've already mentioned the English version of the Sapphic stanza briefly, but it deserves a fuller description. Each line is composed of an amphibrachic foot ( x ′ x ) bordered by trochaic ( ′ x), iambic (x ′ ), and spondaic ( ′ ′ ) feet, with each stanza made up of three lines plus a fourth truncated line to imitate the meter used by the Ancient Greek poetess, Sappho. In the third line, the second foot is spondaic instead of iambic. Here is a scansion of the first stanza of my poem *Moonrise*, which utilizes this complex meter, beautifully fit for intimate, divine, and feminine themes:

′ x | x ′ | x ′ x | ′ x | ′ ′
*Full in the heavens rose the moon with fair tress,*
′ x | x ′ | x ′ x | ′ x | ′ ′
*Blushing behind the clouds, she stood unabashed.*
′ x | ′ ′ | x ′ x | ′ x | ′ ′
*Goddess, gray-eyed Selene, of pearls her white dress,*
x ′ x | ′ ′
*glancing down, she asked:*

Another ode imitating an ancient poet is the English Pindaric ode, inspired by the 5th-century BCE poet Pindar, who was renowned for his poems glorifying victorious athletes of the games held at ancient festivals. The English Pindaric ode mixes various line lengths of iambic feet, with the final hexameter line being the longest. My poems *An Ode to Odysseus* and *Stone-Carved* are both Pindaric odes, suited to evoking a misty ancient past at once heroic and all-too-human. Similarly, the English Horatian ode was derived from Horace, a 1st century BCE Latin poet (who was, in turn, inspired by the poetry of Sappho), echoing his intimate verse in two lines of iambic tetrameter followed by two lines of iambic trimeter in rhyming couplets (AABB). My poem *Facilis Descensus Averno* uses this stanza to evoke the intimacy between a woman and Death, her lover.

### *Other Rhythms & Rhymes*

Several of my poems fall outside of the metrical schemes I've mentioned thus far, and do not necessarily rhyme at the end of the line, if at all. One such rhymeless poem of mine, entitled *P(s)alms*, was written using lines of iambic tetrameter in bi-colons. The inspiration behind this poem and its unique style was the actual Book of Psalms in the Old Testament (also the first book of the third section of the Tanakh). Interestingly, the English word 'Psalms' comes from the Ancient Greek word *psalmoi* (ψαλμοί), meaning 'instrumental music,' eventually associated with the words accompanying them.

Written in Hebrew originally, the lines were not in a strict meter, but rather structured as bi-colons using a feature called *parallelism*, in which each colon contrasts or repeats the other for a prayer-like, emphatic quality. Hence, my poem plays with the subtle contrast in the English language between the words *palms* and *psalms*, and the fact that open palms are often a symbol of prayer. To mimic the delightfully impactful nature of the Hebrew version, which can say a lot with very few words, I used the contrastive iambic foot and split the tetrameter into two cola, which essentially act as dimeters, forcing me to separate the line into sense clauses along the caesura:

*I face my palms   to God above,*
*and pray to Him   my fears abate,*
*along this path   alone I tread,*
*a lonely dirge   I sing my psalms*

Several other poems that also forgo rhyme and meter altogether were inspired by another ancient poetic tradition, namely the poems of Sappho, who has already been mentioned. My first real introduction to Ancient Greek poetry was Mary Barnard's translation of Sappho in sparse, intimate English lines, often incomplete where the papyrus had not survived or when only a few verses had been quoted by a later writer. These fragments, though not reflective of Sappho's poetry in its original state (which would have been composed in strict weighted meter), nonetheless greatly influenced me, partly, I suppose, as symbolic of how fragmentary the voices of women are in the past, and how much of their songs and stories have been lost to the sands of time. The poems marking the start of a new section, namely *Fragmentary Dreams, Fragmentary Night, Fragmentary Doubt,* and *Fragmentary Time*, as their names suggest, resemble Sappho's fragments. On the other hand, the poems *To Aphrodita (Translation of Sappho's Fragment 1)* and the English version of Ἀοίδη, *An Original Lyric Poem in Sapphic Greek,* are translations either directly of Sappho or of an original poem inspired by Sappho. Neither poem rhymes nor follows a strict meter, since they are, after all, translating a language that would not have rhymed its poetry, nor followed accentual meter.

Another type of unrhymed poem I used is the closed-form *sestina* built on a convoluted repetition across stanzas. To mimic the repetitive nature of Spring, I wrote my poem *Spring Again* in this scheme, using iambic pentameter, though any meter can be used. Essentially, the last words of the first six lines, making up a stanza, will be repeated at the line-ends of the rest of the poem in different orders. To visually demonstrate, take the first stanza of my poem:

*It's Spring again and Earth delights* ***anew*** (1)
*when Mother reunites with Daughter* ***dear*** (2)
*and tears of separation dry like* ***dew*** (3)
*as Dawn unfurls and flowers grow in* ***fields*** (4)
*where once a maiden fair was snatched by* ***Death*** (5)
*returned to Life when Winter melts* ***away.*** (6)

The last words of the lines have been bolded and numbered 1 through 6. For the next six lines, the end-words are juggled, changing 1→2, 2→4, 3→6, 4→5, 5→3, 6→1, so that in the next stanza we see:

*Arise and 'ere the break of day* ***away!*** (6)
*Amid the woods and dells sing birds* ***anew*** (1)
*like Phoenixes reborn from ash in* ***Death*** (5)
*and mother bears emerge with younglings* ***dear*** (2)
*while wolves and deer alike now prance in* ***fields*** (4)
*where flower petals bead with morning* ***dew.*** (3)

This revolving of line-end words continues for six stanzas, but the seventh stanza is a three-line envoi combining the six line-end words, putting two on each line (poets differ on the ordering), with the only requirement being that one of them ends the line, like so:

*It's Spring again when wife so* ***dear*** *to* ***Death*** (2, 5)
*returns to* ***fields*** *above now kissed with* ***dew*** (4, 3)
*while far* ***away*** *they sing this song* ***anew.*** (6, 1)

The beauty of a sestina is the creativity required to reuse the same line-end words in a brand new line, at once giving the poem a labyrinthine circularity, but still allowing room for meaningful contrasts where the rest of the line differs. This puzzling poem was invented by Arnaut Daniel, one of the *Troubadours*, a southern European group of lyrical poets who set their poems to simple monophonic music. Once again, we are reminded that poetry, ultimately, was meant to be sung, even if the words carry most of the semantic burden.

The last kind of unrhymed poetry I used was alliterative, namely in *Hymn to Demeter (in Anglo-Saxon Verse), Hymn to Persephone, Death-Bringer,* and *Pearl.* These poems were inspired, as should be expected, by Anglo-Saxon verse, which has already been mentioned above in reference to its accentual meter. *Hymn to Demeter (in Anglo-Saxon Verse)* was written in accented amphibrachal tetrameter, the same meter as *Beowulf* and *Sir Gawain and the Green Knight*, which, instead of rhyming, was *alliterative.* Each line was "divided" in sense, with the weight of meaning on the first half, and the alliteration carrying across this sense divide. Recall the lines of *Beowulf* that we have already seen:

wæs se **g**rimma **g**æst    **G**rendel haten
**m**ære **m**earcstapa    se þe **m**oras heold

The alliteration in bold shows how the same initial consonant sounds *g* and *m* are carried over the line divide, essentially linking them phonetically. Old Norse verse, such as the Poetic Eddas of Snorri Sturluson, goes a step further, not only alliterating across the line but also carrying that alliteration to the first word of the next line, combined with the assonance of syllable sounds within words. Keeping with the Anglo-Saxon tradition, if we take the first four lines of *Hymn to Demeter*, you can see the effect of the meter and alliteration:

x ´ x | x ´ x | x ´ x | x ´ x
*The **m**other of **m**aiden, she **m**ourned for her daughter,*
x ´ x | x ´ x | x ´ x | x ´ x
*by **f**airies in **f**ields far was taken to **f**orests*
x ´ x | x ´ x | x ´ x | x ´ x
*beneath the **d**ark **d**epths of the earth where the **d**ead lie,*
x ´ x | x ´ x | x ´ x | x ´ x
*her **s**orrowful dirges she **s**ang like a **s**pell cast*

In *Hymn to Persephone, Death-Bringer,* I kept the alliteration of Anglo-Saxon poetry, but used the galloping force of the iambic tetrameter and rhyming couplets. This marriage of Germanic and Greco-Roman-inspired poetry styles reflects the relationship my poem draws between the Greco-Roman story of Persephone's descent to the Underworld and the Celtic stories of maidens kidnapped by fairie kings in caves and hillsides. Even the name of the poem joins together the name of a Greek goddess with a typical Anglo-Saxon compound name. Furthermore, both traditions revolve around a young woman borne off in a quasi-death to an eerie underworld, often in marriage to the king of that realm. Both also share the motif of being tricked into eating food and becoming trapped in the "land of faerie" or underworld, then being rescued by someone from the world of the living, usually by striking a bargain with the supernatural King. Both Greco-Roman and Celtic traditions may originate from a common Indo-European myth, or possibly be derived from the ancient Sumerian story where the goddess Ereshkigal is abducted by the primeval dragon Kur and forced to rule the underworld as queen (in fact, the goddess Ereshkigal is mentioned in the poem *The Descent of Ištar into the Underworld,* which retells another Sumerian myth when Ereshkigal is already Queen of the Underworld).

The last poem in alliterative Anglo-Saxon verse and the last poem I will discuss, called *Pearl,* is also, perhaps, my most prized poem in this collection, not just because of its length and complexity, but also because of my experience reading the original Anglo-Saxon poem called *Pearl*, written in the late 14th-century in Middle English (evidently by the same poet who wrote *Sir Gawain*), an experience I can only describe as transcendental. The original poem tells of a father mourning the loss of his pearl in the garden, when he falls asleep and dreams of the 'Pearl-maiden,' a beautiful and majestic figure in heaven, but before he can cross the river to join her, he wakes up. Interpretations—whether the pearl-maiden is his daughter who died young and innocent, or is a symbol for Christianity and its purity—vary, and I do not believe just one is necessary to understand this poem.

Not only is its meaning complex, but the structure itself is astoundingly intricate, and both deserve attention to detail. It is 1212 lines long, with 101 stanzas of 12 octosyllabic lines, each with the rhyme scheme ABABABABBCBC. Not only that, but the stanzas are grouped in sections of five, and within each section, the stanzas are tied together by the repetition of a key "link-word" in the last line of each section, which is then echoed in the first line of the following section. This linking is even accomplished on the level of the poem in its entirety, with the final link-word of the last line of the whole poem being found in the first line at the very beginning.

While I do not pretend my *Pearl* is anywhere near as masterful, I hope my poem can exist in dialogue with the original, reinterpreting the story and telling it through the eyes of a maiden named Pearl (not unlike the *Korē* of the Persephone myth, or *Sofia*, the overarching maiden of this book). To demonstrate the linking between stanzas, take the first three stanzas of my poem:

*Pearl I was named, princess of maids,*
*For lithe my limbs, lovely my locks,*
*Ringlets in white ribbon tied braids,*
*As violins so sweet my vox,*
*Delight in dance, my dress cascades*
*Like water weaves through white-foamed rocks.*
*They ask which eternal god aids*
*A maiden mere, though modest walks,*
*For beauty's blooming blush soon mocks*
*When satin pearl-white skin is stained,*
*Frail and faded beneath my frocks,*
**Gone** *was the Pearl, my girlhood waned.*

*Now younger years have* **gone** *yonder*
*Days of dancing, my girlhood's Dawn,*
*Flower fields my feet did wander*
*Like a maddened, maidenly faun*
*Sun and stars and sky to ponder*
*My limbs light, lithe as a swan,*
*When Time was tiresome to squander,*
*The hours unseen went on and on*
*So delicate they deemed me drawn*
*As pearls are precious, pale and pure*
*In oyster shells their seedlings spawn*
*But once obtained,* **gone** *their allure.*

*Suddenly slipped my pearl,* **gone** *swift*
*From my palm, O pitiful day!*
*As light as wings my legs did lift,*
*Flitting to and fro in fields gay,*
*When I chanced on a childish gift—*
*Narcissus—in naivete*
*I plucked the ploy, pleasure I sniffed,*
*Behold! A trick hid the bouquet,*
*Rapt by him, we rode far away*
*Down to darkness, Death's abode,*
*Leaving the light, I loathed the way*

***Gone** was my pearl on gloomy road.*

*From mother **gone** her maiden dear,*
*A cry was caught on chilly breeze,*
*And lost the pearl in grassy mere,*
*Seized swiftly over endless seas.*
*We came to caverns cold and drear*
*Where dead dwell, dolor and disease,*
*No sun shone this sorrowful bier,*
*No precious pearls do the dead please,*
*No flowers fair, no flitting bees,*
*Save asphodels, their ageless field,*
*No flower, nothing will appease*
*Those doomed to die, the door is **sealed.***

This last stanza marks the end of the first section, and the new linking word, 'sealed,' will link the first stanza of the following section and continue as the new linking word, as we see below:

*My Fate was **sealed**, forgotten there,*
*Just as my pearl from my palm fell,*
*Slipped through a rift, the soil bare,*
*A hallowed grave, the halls of Hell,*
*Where lay my lover in his lair.*
*As pearls sit in their oyster shell,*
*Ever inside their lips ensnare,*
*In such darkling depths did I dwell,*
*Too many terrors there to tell,*
*There I had roamed from room to room,*
*A pearl inside a prison cell,*
***Sealed** inside my shadowy tomb.*

And so on. The last line of the final section's last stanza also ties back to the first line of the entire poem, naming both poem and maiden, echoing the ambiguity of the original Middle English *Perle*:

*...Like the maid, **Pearl**, our poem named.*

***Pearl** I was named, princess of maids...*

If you have a moment, I encourage you to pick a poem from this book, a favorite or at random, or even just one that stuck with you, and read it aloud. Maybe softly chant it or sing the words to a catchy tune—whatever comes to mind will do. Rhythm, after all, can be found in anything if you listen hard enough, from the smallest beat of a metrical foot to the sweeping circles of planetary pathways in this cosmic song we call Life.

ZOE

**ZOË TAVARES BENNETT** is a writer based in Los Angeles, California. She is also the author of the YA romance series *My Sister's Best Friend*, the ancient historical novel *The Sun of God*, a fantasy trilogy, *The Realm of Emmeson*, inspired by Ancient Greek and Egyptian philosophy, and a joint travel essay book, *Imagining the Roman Empire: Essays on Travel & Antiquity in the Mediterranean*. She has a degree in Classics from Williams College, specializing in Ancient Greek and Latin, and is currently a graduate student in UCLA's Proto-Indo-European Studies program.

**www.zoetavaresbennett.com**

Made in United States
Cleveland, OH
17 February 2026

33440899R00071